This book is dedicated to all the children of
this world whose souls are pure, innocent and
full of love and peace, especially Medina,
Haroun and Fareed. It's an honor and
privilege to be your mother.

All the proceeds from this book will be donated to KEI
(Kashmir Education Initiative), a nonprofit organization
dedicated to providing free education and
empowerment to underprivileged children from Jammu
and Kashmir. Please visit their website to learn more or
make a donation at **www.kashmirei.org**.

# Essence of Eid

written by Najmun Riyaz
illustrated by Insha Qazi

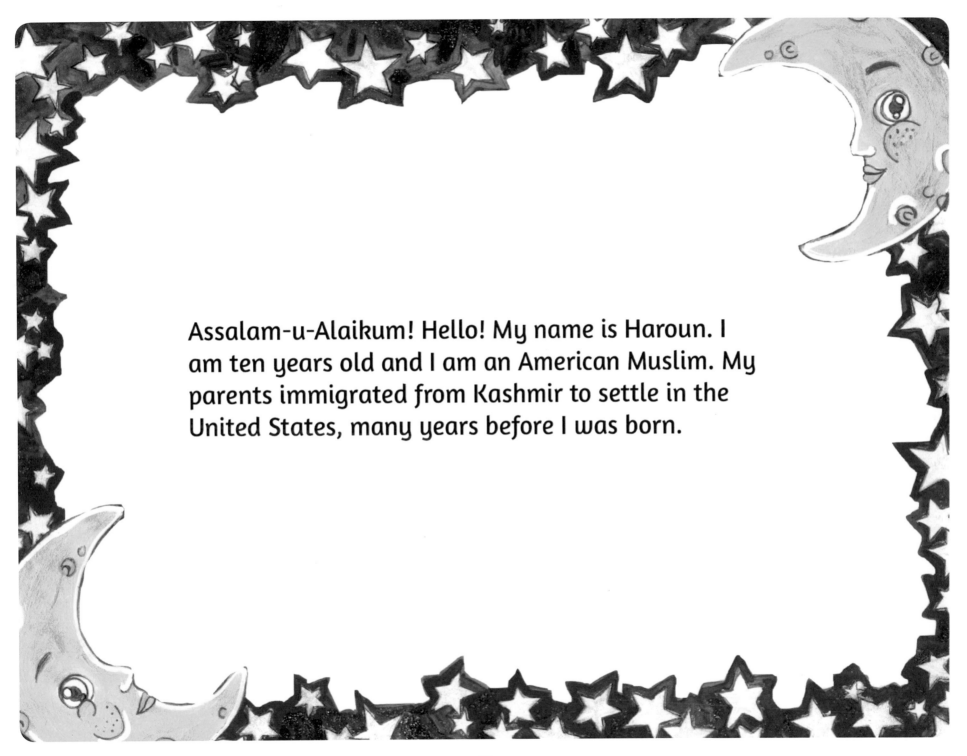

Assalam-u-Alaikum! Hello! My name is Haroun. I am ten years old and I am an American Muslim. My parents immigrated from Kashmir to settle in the United States, many years before I was born.

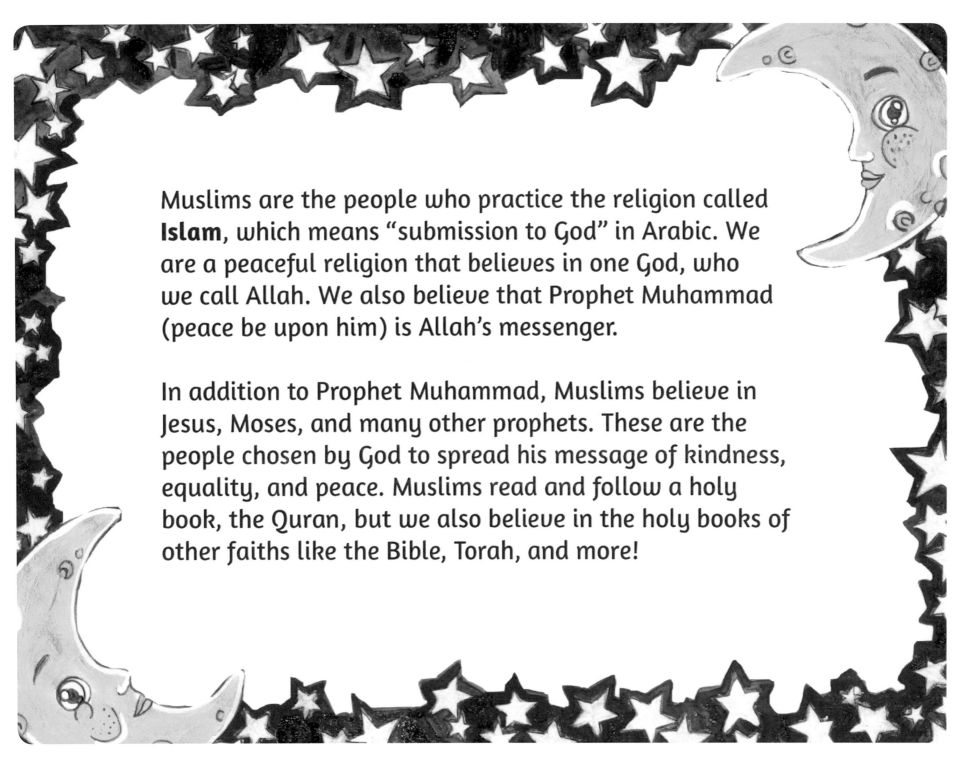

Muslims are the people who practice the religion called **Islam**, which means "submission to God" in Arabic. We are a peaceful religion that believes in one God, who we call Allah. We also believe that Prophet Muhammad (peace be upon him) is Allah's messenger.

In addition to Prophet Muhammad, Muslims believe in Jesus, Moses, and many other prophets. These are the people chosen by God to spread his message of kindness, equality, and peace. Muslims read and follow a holy book, the Quran, but we also believe in the holy books of other faiths like the Bible, Torah, and more!

عيد الأضحى المبارك

عيد الفطر مبارك

Eid ul Adha

Eid ul Fitr

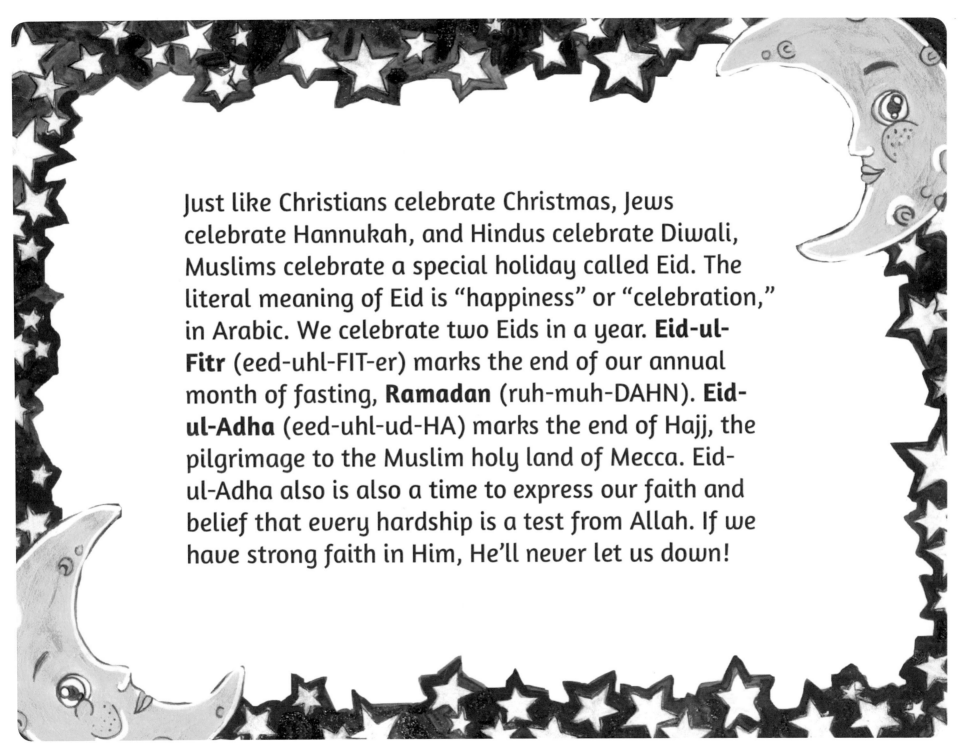

Just like Christians celebrate Christmas, Jews celebrate Hannukah, and Hindus celebrate Diwali, Muslims celebrate a special holiday called Eid. The literal meaning of Eid is "happiness" or "celebration," in Arabic. We celebrate two Eids in a year. **Eid-ul-Fitr** (eed-uhl-FIT-er) marks the end of our annual month of fasting, **Ramadan** (ruh-muh-DAHN). **Eid-ul-Adha** (eed-uhl-ud-HA) marks the end of Hajj, the pilgrimage to the Muslim holy land of Mecca. Eid-ul-Adha also is also a time to express our faith and belief that every hardship is a test from Allah. If we have strong faith in Him, He'll never let us down!

7

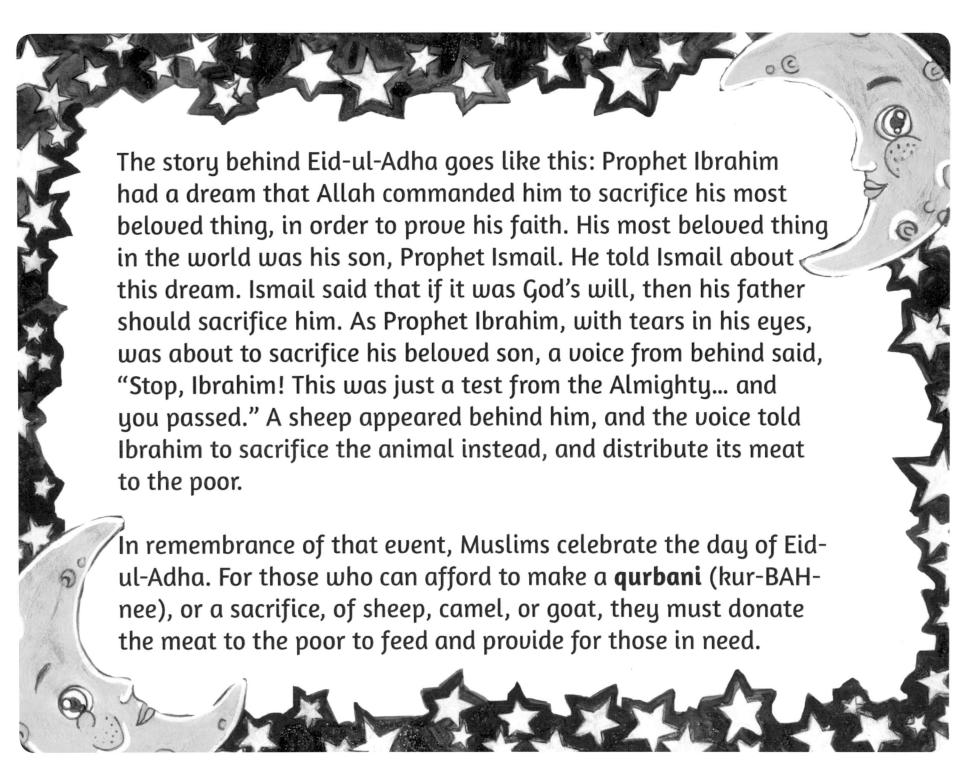

The story behind Eid-ul-Adha goes like this: Prophet Ibrahim had a dream that Allah commanded him to sacrifice his most beloved thing, in order to prove his faith. His most beloved thing in the world was his son, Prophet Ismail. He told Ismail about this dream. Ismail said that if it was God's will, then his father should sacrifice him. As Prophet Ibrahim, with tears in his eyes, was about to sacrifice his beloved son, a voice from behind said, "Stop, Ibrahim! This was just a test from the Almighty... and you passed." A sheep appeared behind him, and the voice told Ibrahim to sacrifice the animal instead, and distribute its meat to the poor.

In remembrance of that event, Muslims celebrate the day of Eid-ul-Adha. For those who can afford to make a **qurbani** (kur-BAH-nee), or a sacrifice, of sheep, camel, or goat, they must donate the meat to the poor to feed and provide for those in need.

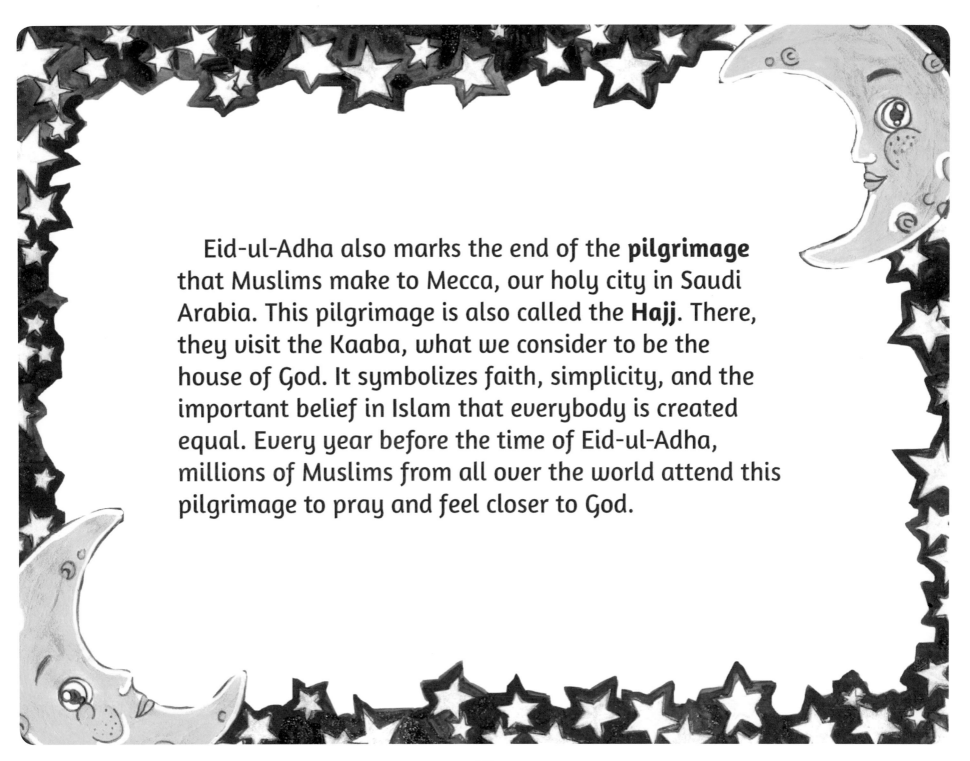

Eid-ul-Adha also marks the end of the **pilgrimage** that Muslims make to Mecca, our holy city in Saudi Arabia. This pilgrimage is also called the **Hajj**. There, they visit the Kaaba, what we consider to be the house of God. It symbolizes faith, simplicity, and the important belief in Islam that everybody is created equal. Every year before the time of Eid-ul-Adha, millions of Muslims from all over the world attend this pilgrimage to pray and feel closer to God.

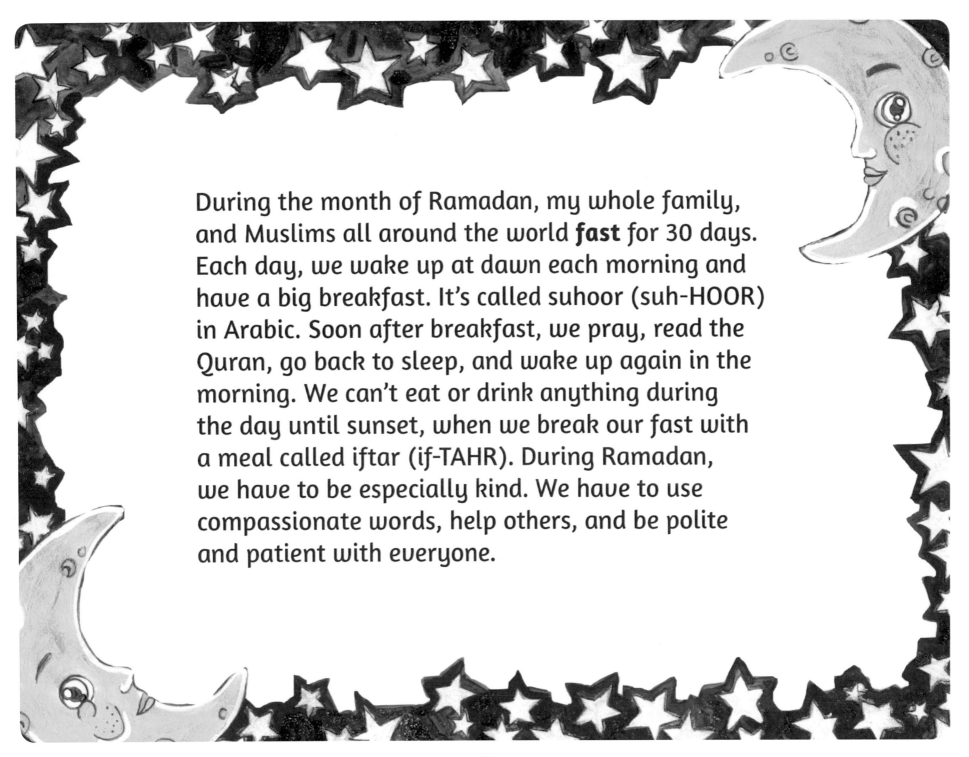

During the month of Ramadan, my whole family, and Muslims all around the world **fast** for 30 days. Each day, we wake up at dawn each morning and have a big breakfast. It's called suhoor (suh-HOOR) in Arabic. Soon after breakfast, we pray, read the Quran, go back to sleep, and wake up again in the morning. We can't eat or drink anything during the day until sunset, when we break our fast with a meal called iftar (if-TAHR). During Ramadan, we have to be especially kind. We have to use compassionate words, help others, and be polite and patient with everyone.

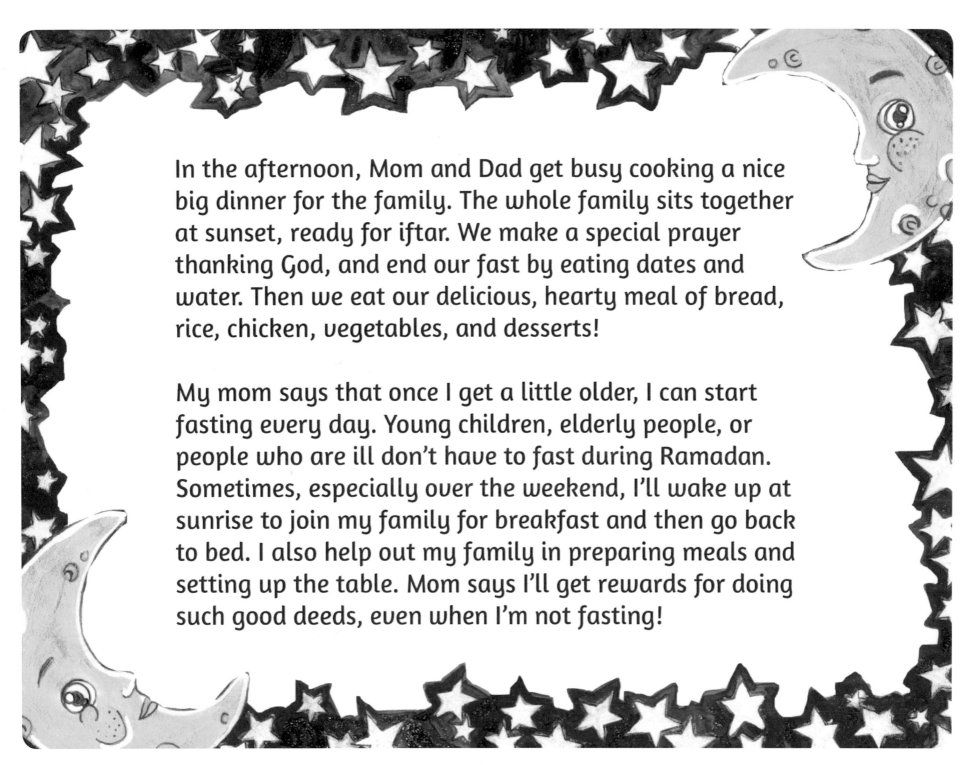

In the afternoon, Mom and Dad get busy cooking a nice big dinner for the family. The whole family sits together at sunset, ready for iftar. We make a special prayer thanking God, and end our fast by eating dates and water. Then we eat our delicious, hearty meal of bread, rice, chicken, vegetables, and desserts!

My mom says that once I get a little older, I can start fasting every day. Young children, elderly people, or people who are ill don't have to fast during Ramadan. Sometimes, especially over the weekend, I'll wake up at sunrise to join my family for breakfast and then go back to bed. I also help out my family in preparing meals and setting up the table. Mom says I'll get rewards for doing such good deeds, even when I'm not fasting!

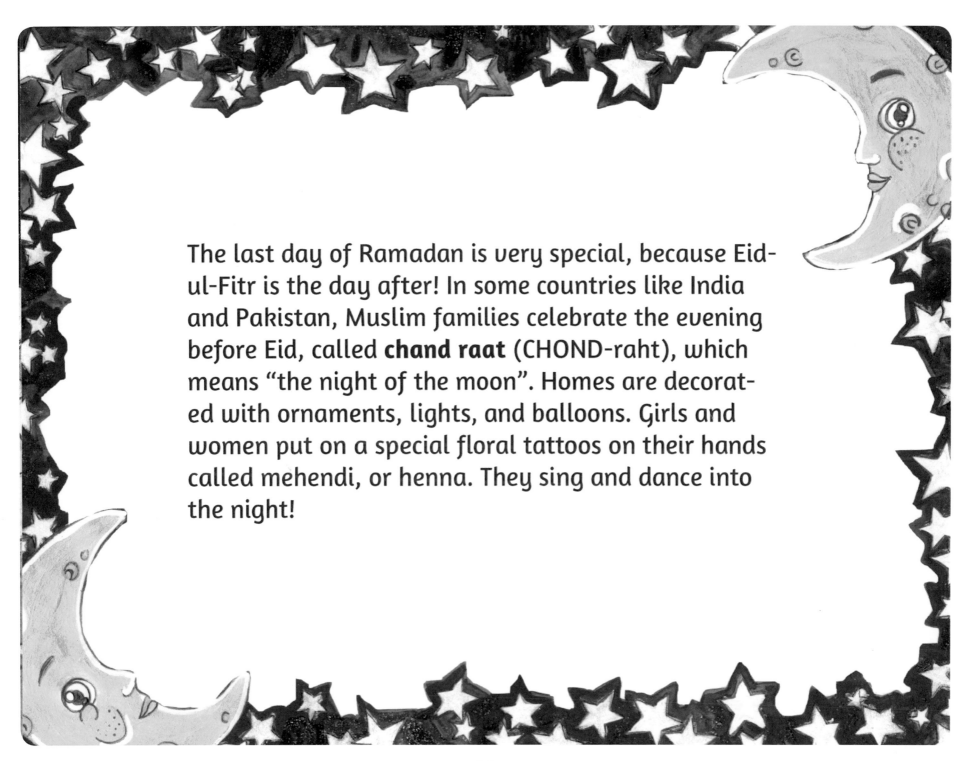

The last day of Ramadan is very special, because Eid-ul-Fitr is the day after! In some countries like India and Pakistan, Muslim families celebrate the evening before Eid, called **chand raat** (CHOND-raht), which means "the night of the moon". Homes are decorated with ornaments, lights, and balloons. Girls and women put on a special floral tattoos on their hands called mehendi, or henna. They sing and dance into the night!

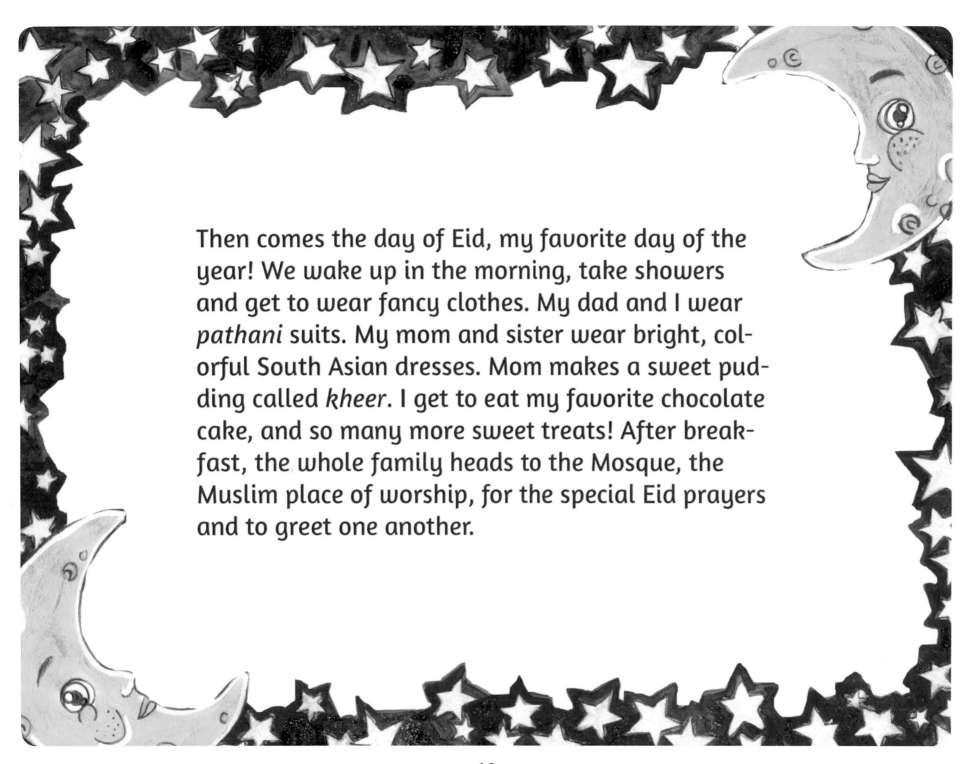

Then comes the day of Eid, my favorite day of the year! We wake up in the morning, take showers and get to wear fancy clothes. My dad and I wear *pathani* suits. My mom and sister wear bright, colorful South Asian dresses. Mom makes a sweet pudding called *kheer*. I get to eat my favorite chocolate cake, and so many more sweet treats! After breakfast, the whole family heads to the Mosque, the Muslim place of worship, for the special Eid prayers and to greet one another.

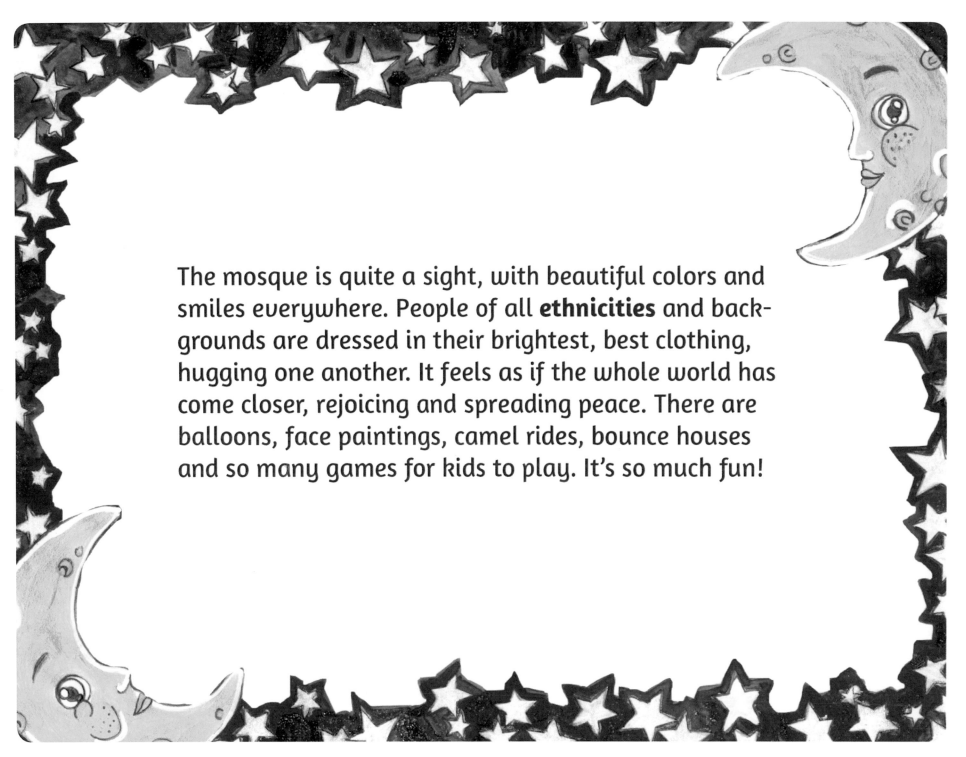

The mosque is quite a sight, with beautiful colors and smiles everywhere. People of all **ethnicities** and backgrounds are dressed in their brightest, best clothing, hugging one another. It feels as if the whole world has come closer, rejoicing and spreading peace. There are balloons, face paintings, camel rides, bounce houses and so many games for kids to play. It's so much fun!

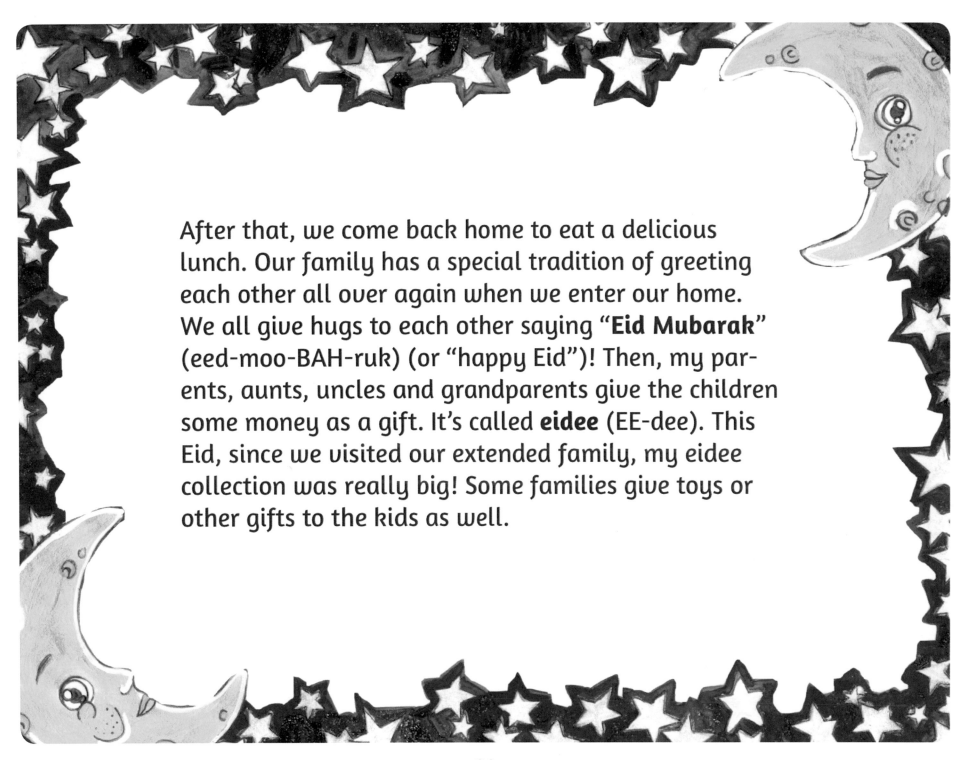

After that, we come back home to eat a delicious lunch. Our family has a special tradition of greeting each other all over again when we enter our home. We all give hugs to each other saying "**Eid Mubarak**" (eed-moo-BAH-ruk) (or "happy Eid")! Then, my parents, aunts, uncles and grandparents give the children some money as a gift. It's called **eidee** (EE-dee). This Eid, since we visited our extended family, my eidee collection was really big! Some families give toys or other gifts to the kids as well.

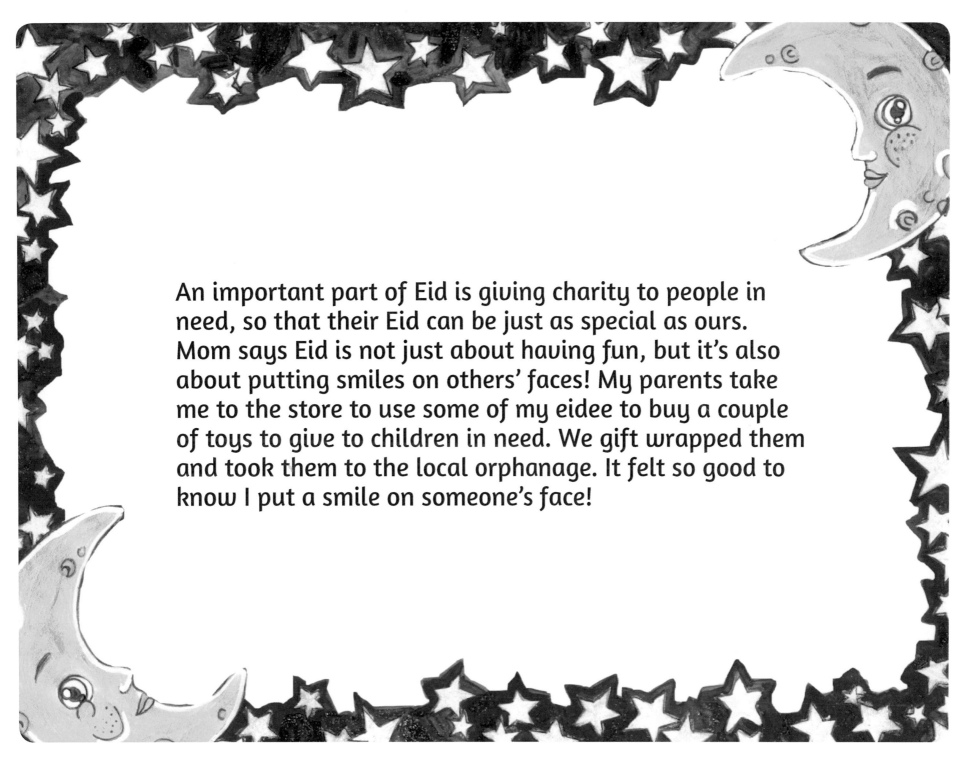

An important part of Eid is giving charity to people in need, so that their Eid can be just as special as ours. Mom says Eid is not just about having fun, but it's also about putting smiles on others' faces! My parents take me to the store to use some of my eidee to buy a couple of toys to give to children in need. We gift wrapped them and took them to the local orphanage. It felt so good to know I put a smile on someone's face!

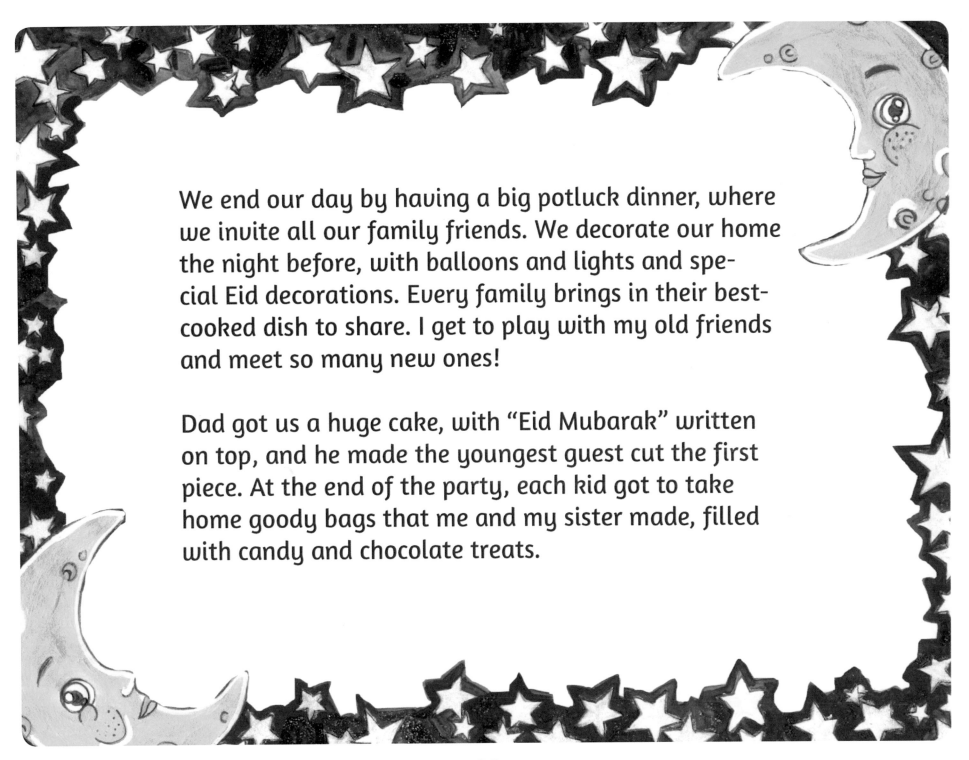

We end our day by having a big potluck dinner, where we invite all our family friends. We decorate our home the night before, with balloons and lights and special Eid decorations. Every family brings in their best-cooked dish to share. I get to play with my old friends and meet so many new ones!

Dad got us a huge cake, with "Eid Mubarak" written on top, and he made the youngest guest cut the first piece. At the end of the party, each kid got to take home goody bags that me and my sister made, filled with candy and chocolate treats.

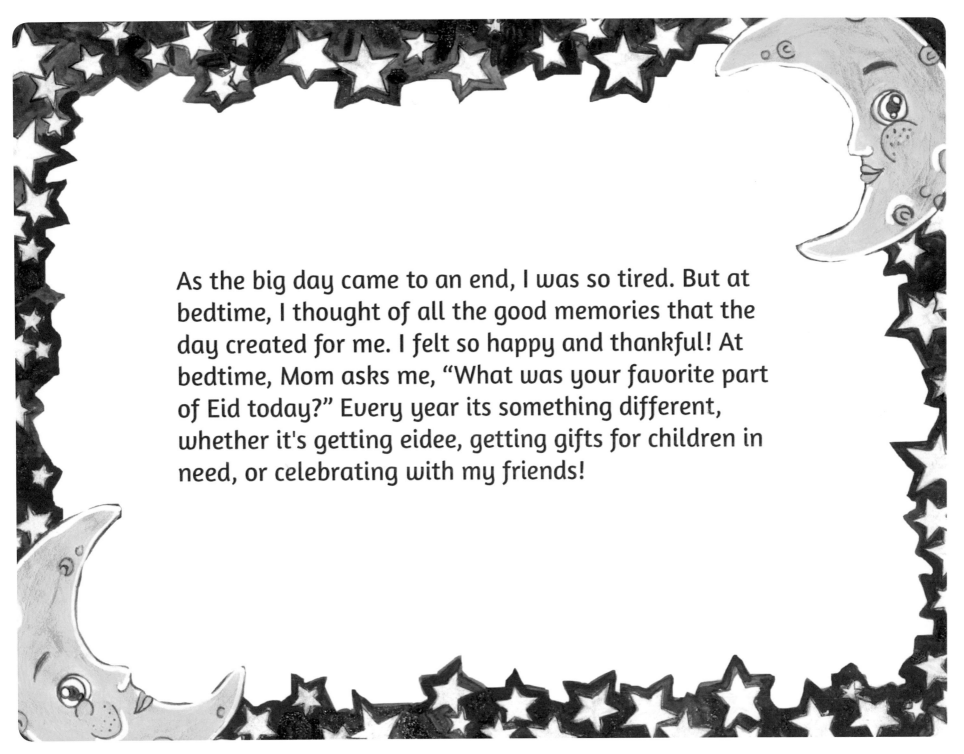

As the big day came to an end, I was so tired. But at bedtime, I thought of all the good memories that the day created for me. I felt so happy and thankful! At bedtime, Mom asks me, "What was your favorite part of Eid today?" Every year its something different, whether it's getting eidee, getting gifts for children in need, or celebrating with my friends!

29

Eid, and every other holiday in all religions and cultures, are all about sharing, showing our love for our friends and family, creating wonderful memories, and above all, being thankful for all the wonderful blessings we have. I can always look forward to saying, "Eid Mubarak!"

# Words to Know

- **<u>immigrate</u>**: to move to another country
- **<u>Islam</u>**: the religion practiced by Muslims as revealed through Prophet Muhammad
- **<u>Eid-ul-Fitr</u>**: a holiday to celebrate the end of Ramadan
- **<u>Ramadan</u>**: the ninth month of the Islamic year, when Muslims fast from sunrise to sunset
- **<u>Eid-ul-Adha</u>**: a holiday to mark the end of the pilgrimage Hajj and to honor Prophet Ibrahim's sacrifice

- **qurbani**: the sacrifice of an animal for the sake of charity on Eid-ul-Adha
- **pilgrimage**: a religious journey
- **chand raat**: a celebration the night before Eid-ul-Fitr; literally meaning "night of the moon"
- **mosque**: a Muslim place of worship
- **ethnicity**: one's belonging to a group that shares national and cultural traditions
- **Eid Mubarak**: a common greeting to celebrate Eid; literally meaning "Happy Eid"
- **eidee**: money gifted to friends and family on Eid

This note was written by Haroun's fourth grade class, after his mom shared the story of Eid with his classmates.

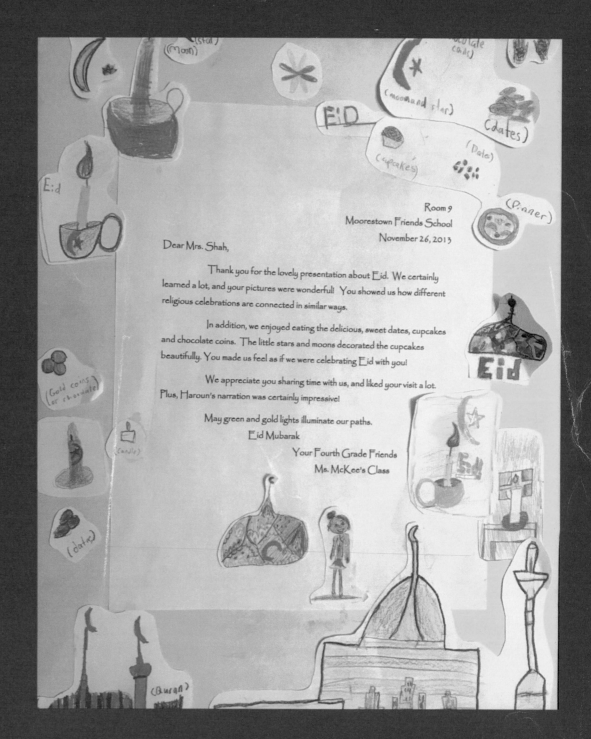